MW01626392

The Finger Lakes

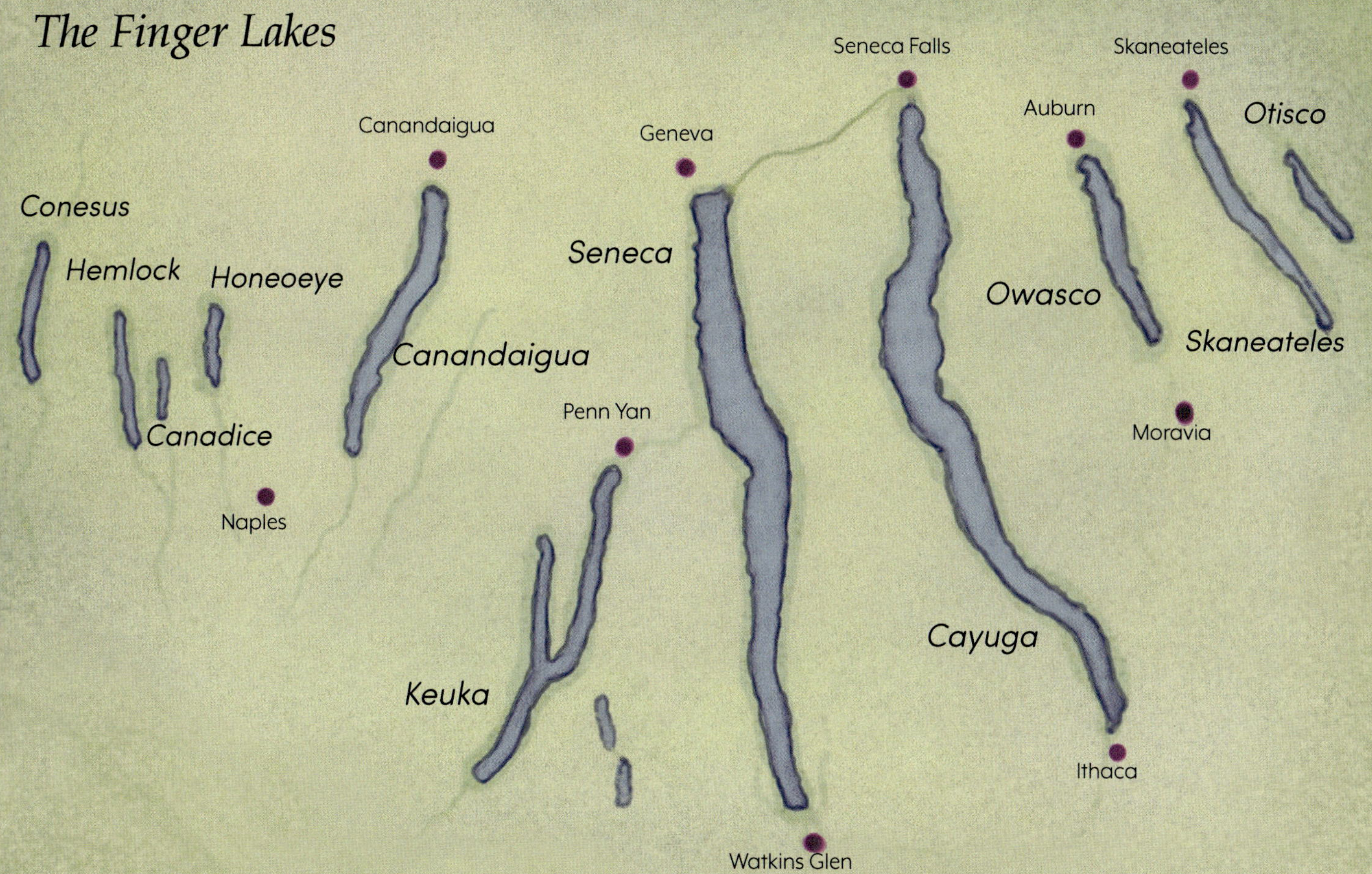

There are eleven Finger Lakes. A well-known regional legend claims the Finger Lakes were formed by the outstretched hands of the Creator or Great Spirit blessing the land. The fingers left imprints which filled with water and became the Lakes. Waterways in the region connect the area with the entire world. The Atlantic Ocean can be reached via Seneca Lake, the Erie Canal and the St. Lawrence Seaway. Other area lakes include the smaller Waneta and Lamoka lakes and Oneida in the East. Millions of years ago, massive glaciers moved through the area carving out deep impressions in the earth. These became the region's lakes, hanging valleys, waterfall gorges and glens.

Canadice (can-uh-dice) Surrounded by steep hillsides, this lake is the highest in elevation, at 1,096 feet above sea level, yet, it is **the smallest Finger Lake**. Only 3 miles long and 95 feet deep, this pristine and mostly undeveloped lake provides drinking water for the city of Rochester.

Canandaigua (can-an-day-gwah) The name means "chosen place." 15.5 miles long, this lake is the 4th largest Finger Lake. It's only 1.5 miles wide. At its deepest point, it is 276 feet deep.

Cayuga (kay-yoo-guh) Cayuga is **the longest Finger Lake** extending to almost 40 miles long (38.15) and 435 feet at its deepest point. It is 3 ½ miles wide at its widest part and the 2nd deepest Finger Lake. A First Nations* name translation is "boat landing." Cayuga Lake has access to the Seneca and Cayuga Canal which connects to the Erie Canal.

Conesus (kuh-nee-shus) is "always beautiful" in a First Nations translation. This lake is smaller and quieter than others . It is 8 miles long from Lakeville to Livonia and only 66 feet deep at its deepest point.

Hemlock (hem-lok) Mostly undeveloped, this lake is a haven for wildlife and sister to Canadice Lake. Twenty-five miles south of Rochester, this lake is a bit over 90 feet deep and only 7 miles long.

Honeoye (hun-ee-oy) Home to the Ring of Fire Tradition, this is the most shallow Finger Lake with its deepest point at 30 feet deep. At only 4.5 miles long, it is the 2nd smallest of the Lakes.

Keuka (cue-kuh) is **one of few Y- shaped lakes** in the entire world. Keuka is the only Finger Lake with an outlet to another Finger Lake. The Keuka Outlet connects Keuka Lake with Seneca Lake. It is almost 20 miles long and 183 feet deep and supplies water to surrounding towns.

Otisco (oh-tis-coh) is 22 miles south of Syracuse and only 6 miles long and 76 feet deep. It's elevation is 788 feet above sea level.

Owasco (oh-wah-sco) is over 11 miles long and 177 feet deep. One translation of its First Nations name is "floating bridge."

Seneca (sen-i-kuh) Seneca is the largest and **deepest Finger Lake.** Named after the Seneca Nation, it is between 35-38 miles long and 618 feet deep.

Skaneateles (skan-ee-at-lis) This long and skinny Finger Lake is 16 miles long and has a maximum depth of 300 feet.

http://www.fingerlakes.org/explore/lakes; https://www.dec.ny.gov/outdoor/32371.html; http://www.priweb.org/;http://wldb.ilec.or.jp/Details/Lake/NAM-17; http://wldb.ilec.or.jp/Details/Lake/NAM-16 * First Nations refers to Native Americans

SENECA LAKE PRESS

Grateful thanks to family, friends and Finger Lakes Locals who have given their support on this journey. Also, thanks to librarians, Kaitlin Bryant (at Belle Sherman Elementary School), Christine Brown (at Waterman Elementary School) and fellow SCBWI author J.M. for editing and reviewing. Special thanks to K.D. (Je t'aime) for her artistic interest and grape illustrations ~ AE

I dedicate each illustrative detail to these Wonderful Women: Clara M., Diane L., Hope G., Liz H., Jodie M., and Sue H. ~ JV

First Edition
ISBN –978-1-7321614-4-3(softcoverCS)

SENECA LAKE PRESS
www.wisforwaterfall.com

1. New York State -Nonfiction. 2. Alphabet Concepts – Juvenile Nonfiction.

3. Finger Lakes Region – Nonfiction. 4. History-United States-Nonfiction

W is for Waterfall

An Alphabet Book of the Finger Lakes Region of New York State

Written by Aileen Easterbrook
Illustrated by Johanna van der Sterre

Aa is for apples, aviation and art
Red and green apples in orchards and carts

Apple orchards are plentiful in the Finger Lakes and the official fruit of New York State is the apple. Apples are celebrated at harvest time with open farm days and events like the Ithaca Apple Festival. Visitors can sample fresh-picked varieties of apples as well as pie, cider, and donuts. Many popular apple varieties like Cortland, Empire, Macoun and Jonagold were introduced by botanists at the New York Agricultural Experiment Station in Geneva. The Lakes provide ideal conditions for farming: a mild climate and healthy soil. Beautiful scenery draws many types of artists to the area. Painting landscapes of hillsides, meadows, lakes, and farms, plein air artists bring the outdoor scenery to life. **If you had wings, where would you fly?** Famous aviators from the Finger Lakes Region include astronaut, Eileen Collins, and pilots, Blanche Scott and Glenn Hammond Curtiss. Curtiss is known for inventing and flying some of the very first airplanes and biplanes.

Bb is for bird watchers with binoculars on boardwalks Searching for blue herons near a bluebird house box

Wetlands in the Finger Lakes are unique and fragile habitats that support many different species of animal and plant life. Montezuma National Wildlife Preserve, north of Cayuga Lake, is a wetland that provides thousands of migratory birds a place to rest, feed and nest. Montezuma is a globally important stop on the Atlantic Flyway, a migratory path used by birds traveling back and forth, to and from, warmer places. Nearby, The Montezuma Audubon Center provides a place to learn about birds, wetland ecology, and conservation.

Montezuma Preserve is visited by over one million (1,000,000) birds each year. The refuge has helped restore threatened bird populations like the Bald Eagle, which was once on the endangered list here in New York. Now, there are several active nests around the park and dozens throughout the State. The refuge provides paths, boardwalks, and binoculars to help visitors spot many different types of birds including osprey, great blue herons, egrets, ducks, shorebirds, and songbirds. In the fall, it's common to spot Canada Geese, flying overhead in a classic V formation. Eagles and osprey build their nests high up in utility poles or treetops. Some nests can be seen year-round.

Cc is for Cayuga Lake, Corning, and Canadice
Paddle past cattails in this lake life paradise

C is for the quiet Lakes west of Keuka: Conesus, Canadice (can-an-dice), and Canandaigua. Conservation is key at Canadice and Hemlock Lakes. Their undeveloped shorelines provide protected places for wildlife to flourish. This, in turn, helps endangered plants, like the Spreading Globeflower, bloom and attract at-risk pollinators like honeybees, Golden-Winged-Warblers and Monarch Butterflies. Canandaigua Lake is calm in places, yet also lively with music and art. Many weddings take place on its northern shore in the town of Canandaigua.

Cayuga Lake is vibrant with the town of Ithaca on its southern shore. Restaurants, boat docks, markets, and Stuart Park are connected by paths for walking and biking around the Lake. The Park is a scenic spot for watching sunsets, having picnics, riding the carousel, fishing, or enjoying a festival. Fields of corn and dairy cows can be found in the surrounding hillsides. Nearby, also beginning with C, is Ivy League college, Cornell University and also, Corning Museum of Glass. Traveling north on the lake, you may encounter Taughannock Falls State Park or the towns of Aurora and Trumansburg. **At almost 40 miles long, Cayuga is the longest Finger Lake.**

Dd is for downhill, where we go in the snow
Racing faster and faster, away we go

Skiing, sledding, and snowboarding are popular outdoor activities during winter. Winter festivals, along with ice skating and hockey, are also popular when the winter season arrives. The Finger Lakes area boasts several ski resorts. Some have vertical drops over 700 feet.

Daring maneuvers on sleds and skis
Moving quickly so we don't freeze

Every year in the town of Skaneateles, people celebrate A Christmas Carol, the classic 19th century tale by author Charles Dickens. The townspeople dress in traditional clothes from England in the 1800's. Women dress in long, wide skirts while men wear full suits and top hats. They sing carols in the gazebo by the lake and act out scenes from the book. **Visitors can join in caroling, take horse-drawn carriage rides, or enjoy delicious, traditional warm drinks like cider and cocoa.**

Ee is for the Erie Canal, a famous inland waterway
Its waters carried people, lumber, grain, coal, and hay

When the Erie Canal first opened in 1825, there were no motors or steam engines to power boats. Instead, non-motorized packet boats were towed by mule and horse power. Attached by a long rope, mules and horses pulled the boats as they walked along on the nearby towpath. The packet boats carried everything from lumber, coal and hay to ice, farm produce, and even people. Smaller canals connected the Finger Lakes to larger cities and greater waterways including the Erie Canal. Many people came to settle in Western New York. Until being replaced by steamships and railroads, the Canal helped people connect and towns thrive through trade and culture. Today, the Erie Canal provides a scenic place for people to enjoy activities like boating and fishing on the historic Canal or bicycling on the Towpath.

Ff is for farm markets like festivals, beyond a morning chore
Instead, a shopping bonanza full of friends, food, and more

Two kids stand on a dock feeding fish. Nearby, a tour boat is waiting to take passengers on a cruise around the Lake. Inside the farm market stands, a woman finds flowers and fruit from a farmer while folk musicians delight a frolicking crowd. In spring, summer and fall, farm markets can be found almost every day of the week in the Finger Lakes. Farmers bring fresh produce, eggs, dairy products, and maple syrup. Artisans bring crafts, jewelry, and local treats, like half-moon cookies. Farm markets bring together communities with regional food and fun. F is also for famous Finger Lakes people like President Millard Fillmore. Visit a replica of his home at Fillmore Glen State Park in Moravia. Astronaut Eileen Collins, Aviator Glenn Curtiss and the National Museum of Soaring have made the Finger Lakes famous for Flight. **National fishing tournaments, along with clean lakes and streams, have made the Finger Lakes famous for fishing.**

Gg is for grapes and gliders that soar, Hand blown glass and so much more

At the Naples Grape Festival, the harvest of grapes is celebrated with all things grape, including juice, wine, jam, jelly, even grape ice cream and especially grape pie! Grape pie makers in Naples make and sell tens of thousands of pies each year. Glass artwork can be found at the festival or nearby at Corning Museum of Glass, which highlights the history of glass-making and contemporary glass artists. Visitors have the chance to make their own glass art. When visiting grape festivals, gorges, glens, and waterfalls are always nearby. At some area gorges and glens, you may catch sight of the elusive **Grey Petaltail Dragonfly.** Their low numbers make them hard to find, but you may find one in their favored habitat - by the cool shady rocks of flowing waterfalls.

Gg is for grapes that grow in our region
At grape harvest time, we celebrate the season

Grape harvests are celebrated at many area vineyards with games, music, horse-drawn hayrides, delicious food, and old-time traditions like grape stomping. **Imagine your bare feet, inside the barrel, grapes squishing between your toes as festive music plays. G is also for gliding. Imagine soaring silently, floating in air currents over the Chemung River Valley, amongst the clouds.** The hobby and sport of soaring through the air on a motorless glider is popular in the Finger Lakes at thhe Harris Hill Soaring Center in Elmira, often called the Soaring Capital of the World. Take a ride or watch from a hillside seat as lightweight gliders are towed off the hill by small planes and left to soar in the air currents. The site is also home to the National Soaring Museum.

Hh is for horses and honey at roadside stands
Hockey on the ice and history across the land

Finger Lakes Hemlock and Honeoye begin with H and so do the towns Hector and Hammondsport. The popular sport of ice hockey is played outdoors on icy ponds, indoors on rinks, at local schools and on professional teams. Throughout the Finger Lakes, horses graze on hillside farms dotted with haybales. Nearby, herons wade in marshy wetlands while beekeepers collect honey for roadside stands. Blue and yellow historic markers and obscure museums tell tales of the region's past. The past and present are well connected to the agriculture surrounding the Lakes. At harvest festivals in spring, summer, and fall, farmers share their bountiful crops with towns and villages. Whether celebrating strawberries, apples, cherries, or tomatoes, potatoes and pumpkins, harvest festivals are full of food and fun. Try propelling a pumpkin into a field of corn, throwing beanbags at a board or getting lost in a corn maze. Face painting, games, rides for kids, entertainment and tasty treats are all part of the community celebration.

Ii is for ice skating and ice hockey played on ice skates
Ice carvings in winter and ice fishing on the Lakes

Long winters are embraced by locals who enjoy activities like ice fishing, ice skating and ice hockey. Ice festivals in winter bring together communities and artists. At the Ice Festival in Ithaca, artists use chainsaws and other carving tools in competitions to create award-winning sculptures from mere blocks of ice. **As people admire ice sculptures, they can enjoy ice cream from a local creamery. What's your favorite flavor? With so many dairy farms in our area, almost every town or village has its own versions of homemade ice cream and unique flavors. Some claim the Ice Cream Sundae was invented here.** During winter, in earlier times, large blocks of ice were cut from the Finger Lakes and used to cool and preserve food. The ice was loaded onto mule or horse-drawn sleds, pulled across the frozen lakes, and moved through the canal system to larger cities. Today, frozen waterfalls in winter are spectacular reminders of how the Finger Lakes were formed. During the Ice Age, glaciers, massive towers of ice, moved through river valleys, carving out deep, clear lakes and hanging valleys where, today, the water falls into streams and gorges, eventually flowing back again into the lakes.

Jj is for Jewels of the Finger Lakes
Local ice cream, tasty milkshakes

A boy Jumps into a glacial lake that sparkles in the sun. Two kids try homemade ice cream from a local creamery. An entertainer juggles colorful objects as festival goers delight in his antics. A band plays upbeat Jazz at an outdoor park. Rare white deer gaze out from their refuge in Romulus. People enjoy expansive views from their lake front porch. There are many Jewels of the Finger Lakes. Some say it's the cool, clear lakes with undeveloped shorelines, like Canadice and Hemlock. Others claim certain waterfalls which glisten with gemstone-like colors in the sunlight, like Rainbow Falls in Watkins Glen State Park.

Sparkling waters, festive fairs
Juggling, jazz and lakeview porch chairs

The herds of white deer that live inside a protected area at South Seneca Army Depot in Romulus are quite a unique sight. Homegrown music enjoyed outdoors on a green park lawn is what some people find most special. Others insist the Jewels are museums of fine art and the art and science of glass in Corning. Whether people are drawn to the peaceful and scenic beauty of the lakes, woods and waterfalls, or the thriving culture of the vineyards, arts, and cuisine, **one thing is certain: with all that it offers, the Finger Lakes Region is a special place.**

Kk is for Keuka Lake, where you can paddle a kayak in a quiet place
Surrounded by hillsides, bejeweled with dazzling colors and open space

At the south end of Keuka Lake is the village of Hammondsport, home to the Glenn H. Curtiss Museum. Hammondsport is known as the Cradle of Aviation because of its hometown hero, Glenn Curtiss, who invented and flew some of the earliest airplanes. Along with biplanes and seaplanes, Curtiss also built and raced some of the very first bicycles and motorcycles. Inventor, pioneer and daredevil, Curtiss has been named the *Father of Naval Aviation* and earned the title, *Fastest Man on Earth*, when, in 1907, **he broke a motorcycle speed record of 136 miles per hour. Every year, the town celebrates the legacy of Curtiss with a Seaplane Homecoming. People gather in the park to ride or watch aquatic airplanes take off and land on the water in Keuka Lake.**

Keuka Lake is one of few Y-shaped lakes in the world. Nestled among steep hillsides and quiet countryside, this lake is unsurpassed in its unique beauty, due to its shape and how its waters flow both north and south. Keuka, a Native American name, was also known by First Nations of the Finger Lakes as Canoe Landing or **Lake with an Elbow.** The Finger Lakes Boating Museum, in Hammondsport, shares the important history of boating in the region and showcases carefully crafted antique boats. Whether in a kayak, canoe or other watercraft, Keuka Lake is an ideal place to go boating.

Ll is for Longhouse, where people lived with their clan
Telling legends and stories of how things began

Long before European settlers came to the Finger Lakes, people were living here in family groups called clans and larger groups of Tribes or Nations. Clan names came from animals like turtle, bear and deer. Twenty to sixty family clan members lived together in one very large, tall and long house. Their homes were quite large with very tall ceilings and lengths ranging from 30 to 300 feet. **The Longhouse, where the clans lived, was warmed by many fires along the center aisle of the longhouse. While adults made food, tools and clothing, children gathered by the fire to listen to important legends, lessons and tales shared by the Storyteller.** One significant story is The Great Law of Peace in which five separate and warring Nations or Tribes united together in peace. This union is often represented by The Hiawatha Belt. It is made with rows of shell beads, or wampum, woven together.

The individual Nations are shown on the belt by lined forms of squares and rectangles with a pine tree at their center. **A beaded white path of peace runs through all the Nations. There are now six Nations but the original five are: Onondaga, Seneca, Cayuga, Mohawk, and Oneida.** The people worked together to provide for each other by fishing, hunting, weaving, gathering food, giving thanks, and sharing respect for the earth. The people have been known as Native American Indians. The French explorers called the united Nations, Iroquois. **Together, they call themselves the Haudenosaunee (Ho-dee-no-SAW-nee), People of the Longhouse**. The game of Lacrosse, played all over the world today, has its roots in upstate New York where the Haudenosaunee have been playing the game for centuries. Today, at Ganandagon in Victor, NY, visitors can see a full-sized Longhouse replica and experience traditional music, art and dance at this cultural center of the Haudenosaunee, one of the original peace villages.

Mm is for Movies

Movies were made here a long time ago
When actors were silent at silver screen shows

What is the oldest movie you've ever seen? Before Hollywood became the center of movie making, Ithaca and the Finger Lakes played a starring role in early movie and film production. From 1912 to 1920, hundreds of film serials were made in the area. Many of those movies were made at a film studio in Ithaca, on the southern end of Cayuga Lake. The studio, Wharton Inc. was started by two brothers, Theodore and Leopold Wharton, who made over one hundred episodes of various film series. To create interesting scenes, filmmakers used some outrageous stunts. In the silent film, "A Prince of India," an actual trolley car was sent over the high Stewart Avenue bridge, careening past Ithaca Falls and crashing into the rocks of Fall Creek Gorge below. Other stunts included burning boats, explosions, and high stakes car races.

Although early films were without spoken dialogue, silent films were not completely silent. Live music was played on piano for special effects or to set a mood. Movies were projected in black and white and referred to as the "silver screen." In 1921, inventor Theodore Case, of Auburn, NY, discovered a way to successfully put sound onto film. **One of those early films with sound was called** *Miss Manila Martin and Her Pet Squirrel*. The film industry brought some alluring stars of the silver screen to the Finger Lakes. Some, like Grace Darling and Irene Castle, dazzled the town with movie star sightings and worldly fashions. Others passed through on their way to greater fame, like Oliver Hardy of the famous comedy duo Laurel and Hardy. Beautiful scenery drew filmmakers to the area, but the region's cold, rain and snow may have driven them to Hollywood, California, the present day, sunny capital of moviemaking.

Nn is for nature centers, near and far
Discover the show, wildlife is the star

Nature Centers in the Finger Lakes open doors to the natural world and allow us to get up close with nature. Centers often have resident animals they care for and offer times where visitors can meet and interact with the animals or ask questions. Outside, walk or hike on wooded trails. Visit butterfly gardens, creeks, or waterfalls. Inside, displays offer games and interesting ways for visitors to discover how all elements in nature work together and rely on each other for survival. Center educators often stress the importance of supporting native wildlife. Native plants, like bee balm, attract native pollinators, like the nine-spotted ladybug, as well as birds, honeybees, and certain butterflies; this, in turn, helps native plants grow and flourish. Some centers, like Museum of the Earth, in Ithaca, share examples of prehistoric world animals including wooly mammoths, pterosaurs, sharks and other fossilized shell animals. **All of the Centers focus on conservation and helping people understand and appreciate the natural world we live in.**

Oo is for Owasco Lake and Lake Otisco too

Swim or sail, skip rocks of shale, on lakes so calm and blue

Towns near Owasco Lake have much to offer. The town of Auburn, at the north end of the Lake, has many cultural and historic sites as well as a thriving theatre scene. See a show at the Merry-Go-Round Playhouse in Emerson Park. Visit the historic Seward House Museum. Auburn is also home to the Case Research Lab where Theodore Case discovered a way to put sound on films. This birthplace of talking movies is housed in the Cayuga Museum. Nestled amongst the hills, south of Owasco Lake, in the town of Moravia, is Fillmore Glen State Park. Here you can hike miles of trails, swim near a waterfall, or visit a 19th century replica of a log home belonging to the 13th President, Millard Fillmore, who was born here. **Nearby, in the town of Ithaca, is the Lab of O, a nickname given to Cornell's Lab of Ornithology; here you can listen to different bird calls, walk the trails, or see birdlife in action through a large viewing window.**

Pp is for Penn Yan

Penn Yan is a town north of Keuka Lake
Once it was home to the world's largest pancake

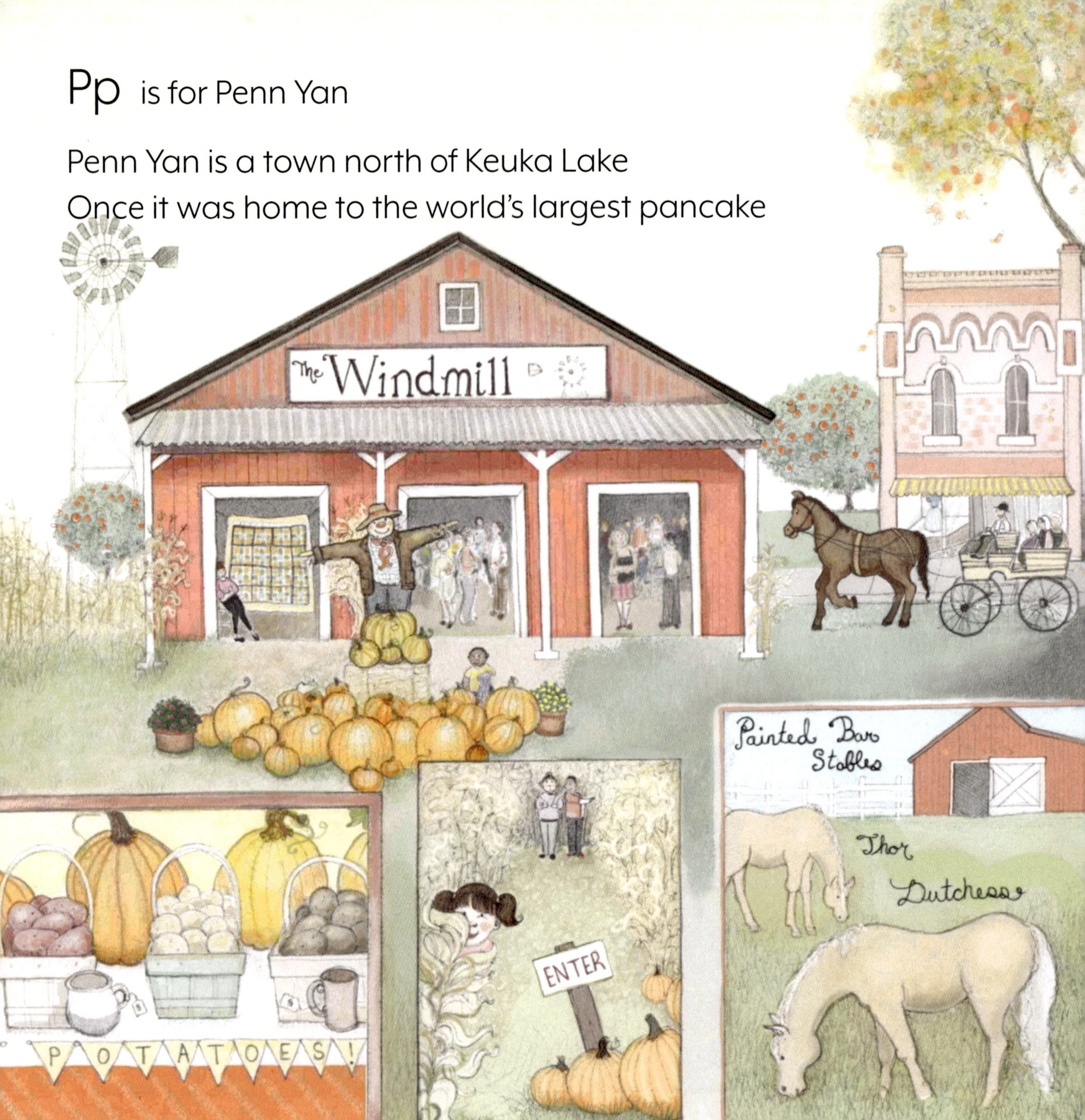

On the northern points of Y-shaped Keuka Lake are the towns of Penn Yan and Branchport. Penn Yan is home to The Windmill Farm and Craft Market. There, you can find pottery and produce including peaches, pumpkins, potatoes and preserves. Popular fall activities in the region include open farm days that offer corn mazes. Wind your way through corn stalks, get lost, then use clues to help you find your way out. **Farms with horses are plentiful in the area. If you enjoy riding, you might take a trail ride on a Pinto or Palomino at a local stable.** In Branchport, you can find The Finger Lakes Museum and Aquarium. The Museum is dedicated to conservation efforts and exploring natural history through field experiences like hiking and paddling. Higher education in an idyllic Finger Lakes setting can be found at nearby Keuka College and Hobart and William Smith Colleges.

Plein Air artists painting landscapes in the park
Playgrounds, pancakes, and a storied town landmark

In 1987, at the annual Birkett Mills Buckwheat Harvest Festival in Penn Yan, the Mill and the town broke a world record for making and baking the World's Largest Pancake! Festival goers were offered pieces of the enormous pancake for one dollar a piece. The pancake was over 27 feet across, topped with 15 pounds of maple syrup and 68 pounds of butter from local dairies. A cement mixer was used to stir the batter. A construction crane was used to flip the pancake and people used a garden rake to spread the butter on this pancake that weighed over 4,000 pounds! The record was surpassed several years later but today, mounted onto the Birkett Mills building, the very large pan in which the record making pancake was made remains in town as a reminder of this great feat.

Qq is for Quest, Quirky and Quaint

Go on a quest to find quiet woods, quirky shops and quaint little towns
Take scenic drives and scenic rides or see high energy racing on roads all around

Scenic byways, roads, and routes lead to unique places where visitors can discover hidden treasures: antiques, regional arts, like at the Corning Museum of Glass, cafes, local crafts and charming shops. **A horse and buggy are a common sight on country roads where traditional communities live and farm.** Beyond farmlands, towns, and villages, forests and secluded woodlands await trail explorers in preserves, in State Parks, on the Finger Lakes Trail and in the Finger Lakes National Forest.

Rr is for Racing and Roads

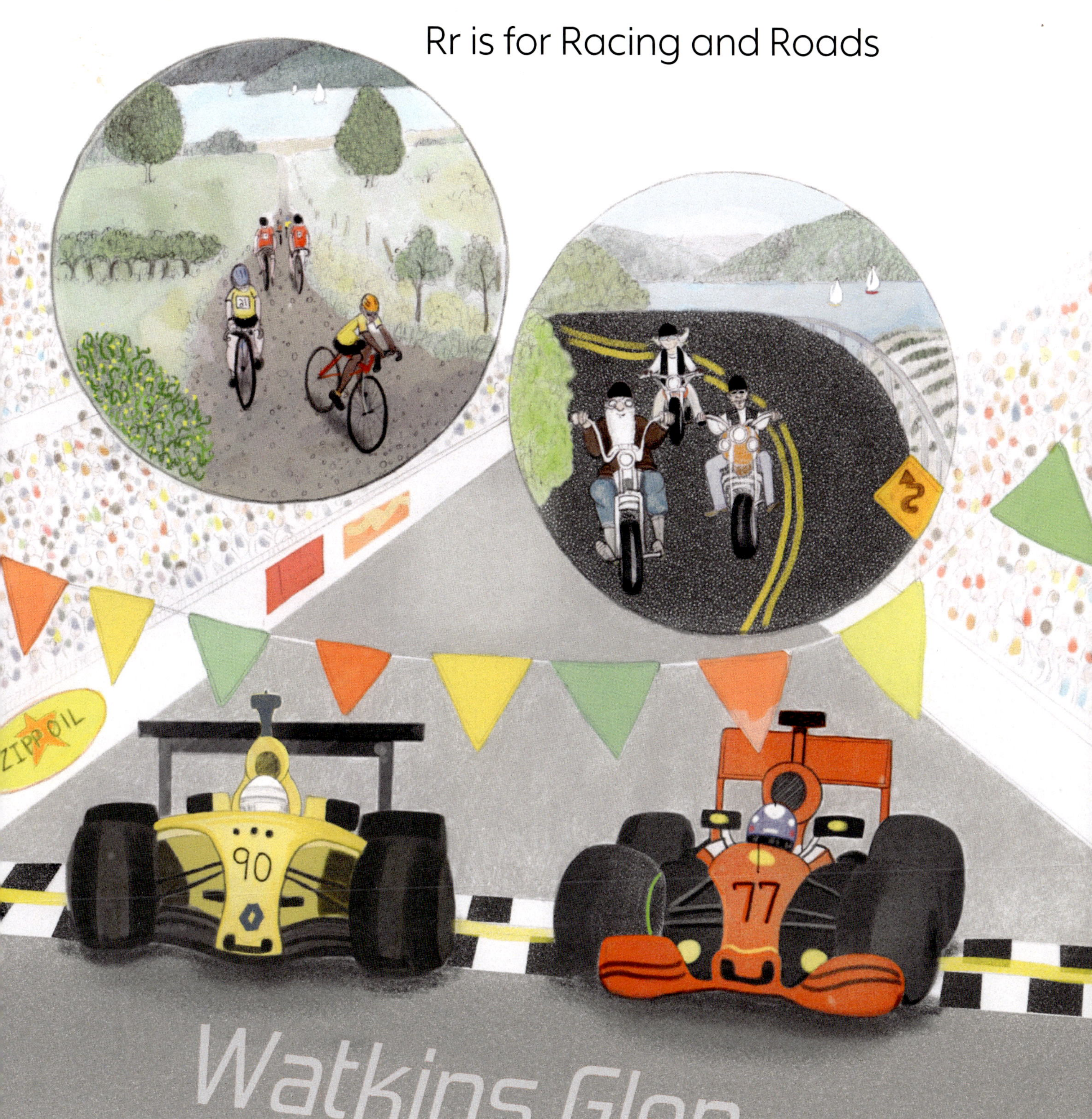

Beautiful scenery of the Finger Lakes attracts road enthusiasts of all types: vintage car owners, people who take day trips, and those who ride motorcycles and bicycles. In Watkins Glen, there is a long tradition of racing and motorsports. At Watkins Glen International, a world-class motor speedway, race car drivers compete for championships. **Crowds fill the stands, awaiting a winner. The flag comes down to signal the start of the race.** Drivers must maneuver challenging courses and tricky turns at high speeds as they race toward the finish line. The Glen has been home to many major racing series including NASCAR, IndyCar and Formula One Grand Prix. The Glen draws both local and international crowds and is often regarded as the birthplace of American Road Racing.

Ss is for Seneca Lake, Skaneateles, Sturgeon & Salt

At the Southern end of Seneca Lake, water sparkles in the setting sun
Sailboats cruise by, people stroll the pier, a forever haven of tranquility and fun

The Watkins Glen waterfront, at the south end of Seneca Lake, is often a busy and energetic place. Live music plays, kids frolic, and adults relax along the pier while taking in scenic views. Some enjoy the views from their boats at the marina, others from vineyards, restaurant seating or tour boats and dining cruises. This bustling waterfront hosts fishing derbies, weddings, sailboat regattas and, even, cardboard boat races! The waterfront is also home to Lakeside Park, which has playgrounds, a skate park, and areas for picnics, cookouts, swimming, and camping. Often referred to as the "Heart of the Finger Lakes," Watkins Glen is also known for motorsports racing and the myriad of waterfalls and rock formations at Watkins Glen State Park.
Reaching depths of over 600 feet, Seneca Lake is the deepest of the Finger Lakes. Sturgeon, some of the largest freshwater fish, live in the Lakes. Sturgeon found in Seneca Lake can weigh up to 100 pounds.

The Finger Lakes region has a long history of salt production. Plentiful amounts of salt can be found deep below the surface of the Finger Lakes. Left behind by an ancient sea that used to cover the Lakes, salt was originally mined from Onondaga Lake, north of Syracuse. So much salt was produced here that Syracuse came to be known as "Salt City." Today, you can revisit the history of salt in our region at Liverpool's Salt Museum, 5 miles from Syracuse. Salt mines remain on both Cayuga and Seneca Lakes, with some mines reaching over 1,000 feet below the surface of the Lake. Also beginning with S is Skaneateles (skan-ee-at-e-les or skinny-atlas), a charming village that hosts boat shows and the holiday-time Dickens Festival. The village is at the north end of Skaneateles Lake. Known as one of the cleanest Finger Lakes, this pristine Lake is 16 miles long.

Tt is for Trout, Trails & Trumansburg

Follow Trails to Trumansburg, find brown trout in a stream
Find turtles at Taughannock, know Harriet Tubman's freedom dream

In the town of Trumansburg, you can visit a waterfall taller than Niagara Falls. Taughannock Falls is the tallest waterfall with a single freefall drop in New York State. This impressive waterfall plunges 215 feet down. Its waters travel through gorges and streams, emptying out into the lake, where fishing for trout is popular pastime. **Lake Trout are the most common type of trout found in the Lakes, but other area trout include: Rainbow, Brown and Brook.** In the 19th century, you may have found abolitionist Harriet Tubman telling tales on the Underground Railroad, which helped transport slaves to freedom. Tubman, who escaped slavery herself, was known as the "Moses of her People" because she guided dozens of slaves toward freedom. Trails in the Finger Lakes lead to interesting places, all connected by common themes. Find local artists, cheese and ice cream makers, historic sites, hiking paths, museums and more.

Uu is for Unique places and U-Pick stands and farms
Scenic country roads and small-town country charms

Driving along country roads, it's simple to find plentiful signs for produce stands and U-Pick sites. **U-pick farms allow visitors to choose their own produce from ripe fruit trees or rows of berries. Pick strawberries, cherries or apples. Pick a pint, a quart or bushel. Enjoy them on the spot or take them home to make jellies, jams and pies.** U is also for the Underground Railroad, a network of people and places that helped slaves escape to freedom. Many people in the Finger Lakes assisted the Railroad by providing stations, or safe houses, to protect the runaways on their journey. Slaves often traveled secret routes at night. **They followed a star constellation called the Drinking Gourd that includes the North Star.** Later in life, with help of Senator William Seward and family, Harriet Tubman established a home for herself and freed slaves who needed care and rest. Visitors can explore her homestead, a National Historic Park, in the town of Auburn.

Vv is for valuable women, victorious in their fight
To have their voices heard and gain equal rights

In 1848, women were not allowed to vote. In July of that year, however, 300 people came together at the first women's rights convention, in Seneca Falls, to try to change this and other unfair laws. They drew up the Declaration of Sentiments, a document that, along with a women's right to vote, called for basic civil and human rights for all people. The voting law did not change for a long time. **With the passing of the 19th Amendment to the Constitution, in 1920, seventy years after the convention, women citizens gained the right to vote.** The Women's Rights National Historical Park in Seneca Falls tells the story of the Convention and women's struggle to gain equal rights. Nearby, at Stanton Park, a lifelike statue, by local sculptor Ted Aub, honors three prominent area leaders in the Women's Rights Movement and their meeting before the Convention: Susan B. Anthony, Amelia Bloomer and Elizabeth Cady Stanton.

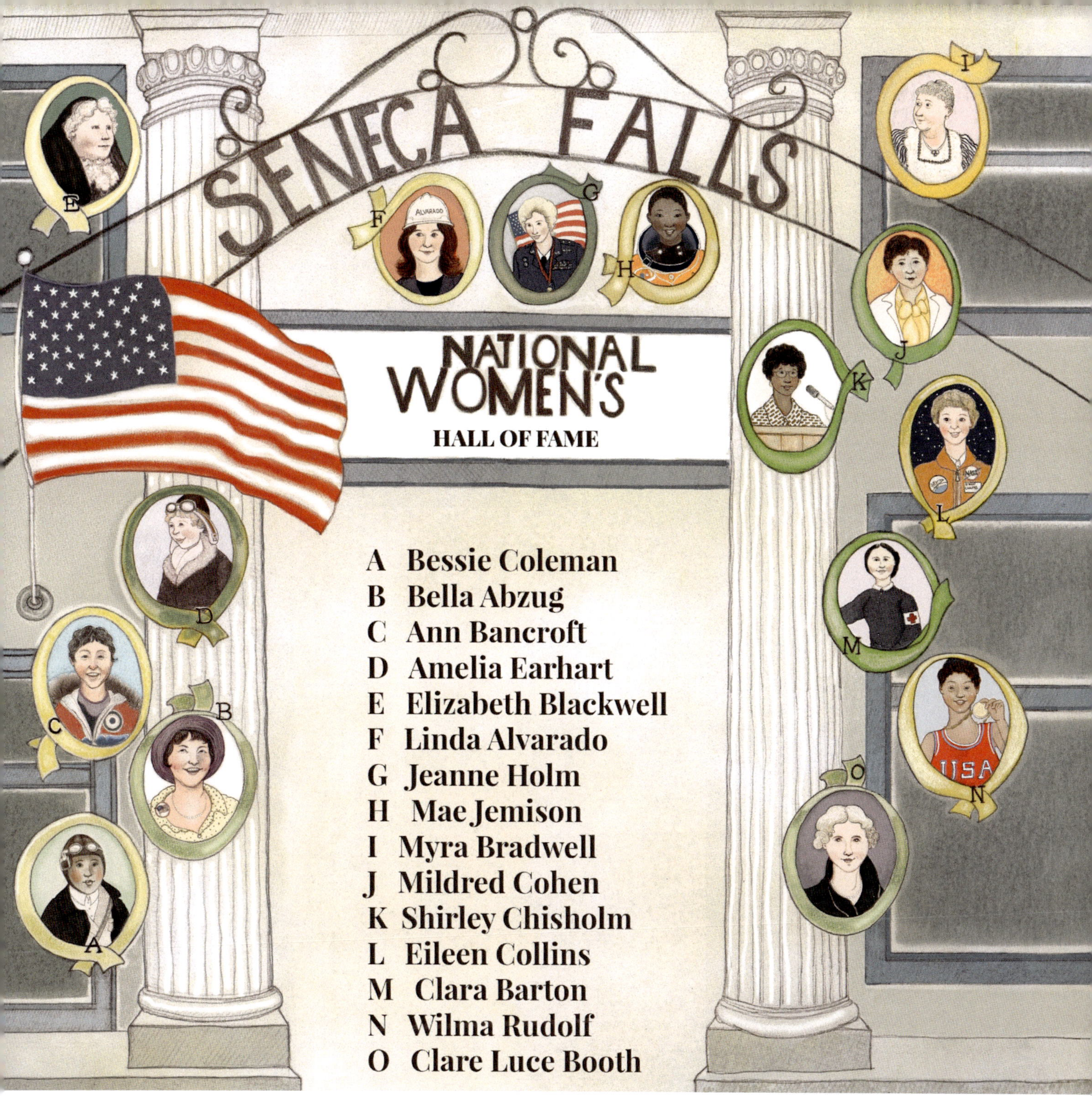

Seneca Falls is often called the birthplace of the Women's Movement. It is also home to the National Women's Hall of Fame (NWHF). The NWHF acknowledges the vast contributions American women have made in many areas. Despite facing harsh opposition to women's participation, women have succeeded in a wide variety of fields including: Medicine, Music and Law; Athletics, Aviation and Art; Education, Engineering and Science; also,the Military and Technology. One 19th century woman, Elizabeth Blackwell, was refused entry from many medical schools on the basis of being a woman. Despite her challenges, she persisted and was accepted to a medical school in Geneva, New York, Hobart College. In 1849, she became the first woman to earn a medical degree. After years of hard work in the military, Jeanne Holm became a two-star General. In 1999, local astronaut, Eileen Collins, became the first woman to command a space shuttle mission. **Every year, new women are inducted into the Hall of Fame. Perhaps you, or someone you know, could be the next inductee!**

Ww is for Waterfalls

Waterfalls wander and wind over stones
Tumbling down over prehistoric bones

Many people visit the Finger Lakes to see and admire the multitudes of magnificent waterfalls. Of the hundreds of waterfalls in the area, some are quiet, trickling like streams, while others are roaring and powerful like Hector Falls outside of Watkins Glen. Named for its milky color, Buttermilk Falls, in Ithaca, is a popular swimming spot. Rainbow Falls, in Watkins Glen State Park, draws hundreds of thousands of visitors each year to witness waterfall droplets, bright as colorful jewels, as sunlight strikes the falls. Here, people climb winding stone staircases and walkways leading to seemingly endless new waterfalls, streams, reflection pools and rock formations, each exhibiting a unique beauty different from the last.

Taughannock Falls, within Taughannock State Park, next to Cayuga Lake, towers above a gorge trail with an impressive 215-foot vertical drop. This is the tallest single-drop waterfall in New York State. It is even taller than Niagara Falls! If you find yourself walking along the quiet village Streets of Montour Falls, you may come across the tumbling waters of She-Qua-Ga Falls. **The French King, Louis Phillippe, the XVIII, once visited the area. It is rumored that he sketched the Falls and that his sketch can now be found in the famous Louvre Museum in France.** Constant moving water and glacial activity have churned up many fossils in our creeks and gorges making it possible to find fossils from an ancient sea. Many fossils found in creeks and gorges, have been dated to the Devonian Period, over three hundred million (300,000,000) years ago.

Xx is for eXcellent schools and sports teams
Animals now eXtinct housed in museums

Esteemed colleges and universities make their homes in the Finger Lakes. Many have teams that eXcel in sports and compete in both national and state championships. **Cheer at an Ivy League football game, see crew teams row on the canal, attend a high energy hockey or lacrosse match.** College students come here to study ecology, engineering, education, business, medicine, music and more. They bring youthful energy and world culture to our small towns. Locals are fortunate to have the great food, music, art and innovation that thrives in this environment. Outstanding schools are matched by eXcellent museums. Many have eXciting hands-on eXhibits to eXplore like the science museums in Ithaca and Syracuse or the Museum of Play in Rochester. **At the Museum of the Earth in Ithaca, eXplore natural history, dig for fossils, and see Amelia, a life size replica of a Jurassic pterosaur with a 36-foot wingspan.**

Yy

Near a pond with lilies, hidden in the woods, songbirds sing notes sweet and high
Unlike the Yellow-Bellied Sapsucker who taps instead and begins with letter **Y**

Nestled near neighborhoods, highways and even a busy airport, is a sanctuary for birds and other wildlife, Sapsucker Woods. Sapsucker Woods are connected to Cornell's Lab of Ornithology – a place for the study and research of birds.The Woods were named in 1909 when two bird enthusiasts, Arthur Allen and Louis Agassiz Fuertes, were surprised by a rare sighting, a nesting pair of yellow-bellied sapsuckers. At the time, these birds were rarely found in this area. Today, with the growing protection of woodlands, they are a common sight. **Members of the woodpecker family, yellow-bellied sapsuckers find food by using their sharp beaks to poke small, shallow holes in trees. The holes are full of sap and insects, which they pick up with their brush-like tongues.** Some songbirds you may encounter at Sapsucker Woods include: robins, cardinals, chickadees, finches, and bluebirds. Bluebirds are the official bird of New York State.

Zz is for Zebra Mussels

Zebra Mussels are sharp and rough on tender feet
Yet these tiny shellfish, filter water as they eat

Zebra Mussels are tiny shellfish that came to the Finger Lakes in the 1980's, by hitching rides on the bottom of large ships coming from the Atlantic Ocean and through the Great Lakes. As you may have guessed, Zebra Mussels are named for their striped shells. Zebra Mussels spread rapidly, laying up to one million (1,000,000) eggs per year! They compete for food sources with native fish, like trout, and can do severe damage to boats. On a positive note, Zebra Mussels are filter feeders and they improve lake clarity by removing particles from the water. In some parts of the lake, it's possible to see 30 to 40 feet down to the very bottom of the lake. The clear water helps certain fish lay more eggs. High above the lake bed, people can be found swimming, fishing, having picnics, and enjoying life in the Finger Lakes.

Index of Places and Subjects

(in words and pictures)

Further Reading and Resources

Art http://www.fingerlakespleinair.com; http://arttrail.com/portfolios.html; https://www.cmog.org/programs; https://www.chemungvalleymuseum.org; https://rockwellmuseum.org; http://www.museum.cornell.edu; http://everson.org/; http://new.artizanns.com/;http://www.handwork.coop/

Agriculture and Open Farm Days http://www.ironkettlefarm.com/; http://www.picknpatch.com/; http://www.stoughtonfarm.com/; http://www.varickwinery.com/events/cherry-festival; Ward O' Hara Agricultural Museum

Aviation, Glenn H. Curtiss, Soaring and Gliders https://www.glennhcurtissmuseum.org; https://www.soaringmuseum.org; http://www.wingsofeagles.com/

Birds https://www.allaboutbirds.org; https://www.allaboutbirds.org/guide/Yellow-bellied_Sapsucker; http://www.cayugabirdclub.org/where-to-bird; http://www.audubon.org/atlantic-flyway; https://onondagaaudubon.com/birding/birding-how-to-get-started; https://www.fws.gov/refuge/Montezuma/visit/plan_your_visit.html

Boating and Fishing https://www.flbm.org; http://www.acbs-flc.org/boatshow; http://sampatch.org; https://midlakesnav.com; https://www.laketroutderby.org/; https://www.senecaharborstation.com; http://www.thewaterfrontfestival.com

Erie Canal and Waterways https://eriecanalmuseum.org; http://senecamuseum.com; http://sampatch.org; https://www.cmog.org/glassmaking/demos/hot-glass-demos/glassbarge; https://eriecanalway.org/learn/history-culture; http://senecamuseum.com/

Finger Lakes (General) https://www.fingerlakesmuseum.org/; https://www.lifeinthefingerlakes.com/; http://www.sunnydaysny.com/; http://www.visitfingerlakes.com/; http://iloveflx.com/;http://www.fingerlakes.com

Haudenosaunee http://www.ganondagan.org

Movie and Film History https://whartonstudiomuseum.org/wharton-studio-history; http://cayugamuseum.org/case-research-lab

National Sites http://www.cnyhiking.com/FingerLakesNationalForest.htm; https://www.soaringmuseum.org/; https://rockwellmuseum.org/; https://www.theglen.com/?homepage=true; https://www.nps.gov/hart/index.htm; http://www.nyhistory.com/harriettubman/home.htm

Nature Centers http://www.rmsc.org/cumming-nature-center; http://www.tanglewoodnaturecenter.com/; http://www.priweb.org/index.php/education/cayuga-nature-center; http://www.limehollow.org/; http://www.onondagacountyparks.com/parks/beaver-lake-nature-center/

Road Racing http://www.racingarchives.org

Trails: Hiking, Biking, Birding, & Road Trips http://fingerlakestrails.com/especially-for-kids; http://www.fltconference.org/trail; http://www.fingerlakes.org/outdoors/hiking-biking; http://www.fingerlakes.com/activities/biking/insiders-guide; http://www.newyorkupstate.com/finger-lakes/2015/09/best_fall_drives_in_the_finger_lakes_region.html; https://www.keukaoutlettrail.org; http://fingerlakestrails.com/finger-lakes-sweet-treat-trail/

Waterfalls and State Parks http://www.visitithaca.com/attractions/taughannock-falls-state-park; http://nyfalls.com/waterfalls/watkins-glen/; http://nyfalls.com/waterfalls/fillmore-glen-state-park/

Watkins Glen http://www.thewaterfrontfestival.com; https://www.senecaharborstation.com; https://www.watkinsglenchamber.com/

Women's Movements https://www.womenofthehall.org/; https://www.history.com/topics/seneca-falls-convention; http://www.newyorkupstate.com/seneca-falls/2015/05/womens_rights_national_historical_park.html

Made in the USA
Monee, IL
28 October 2020